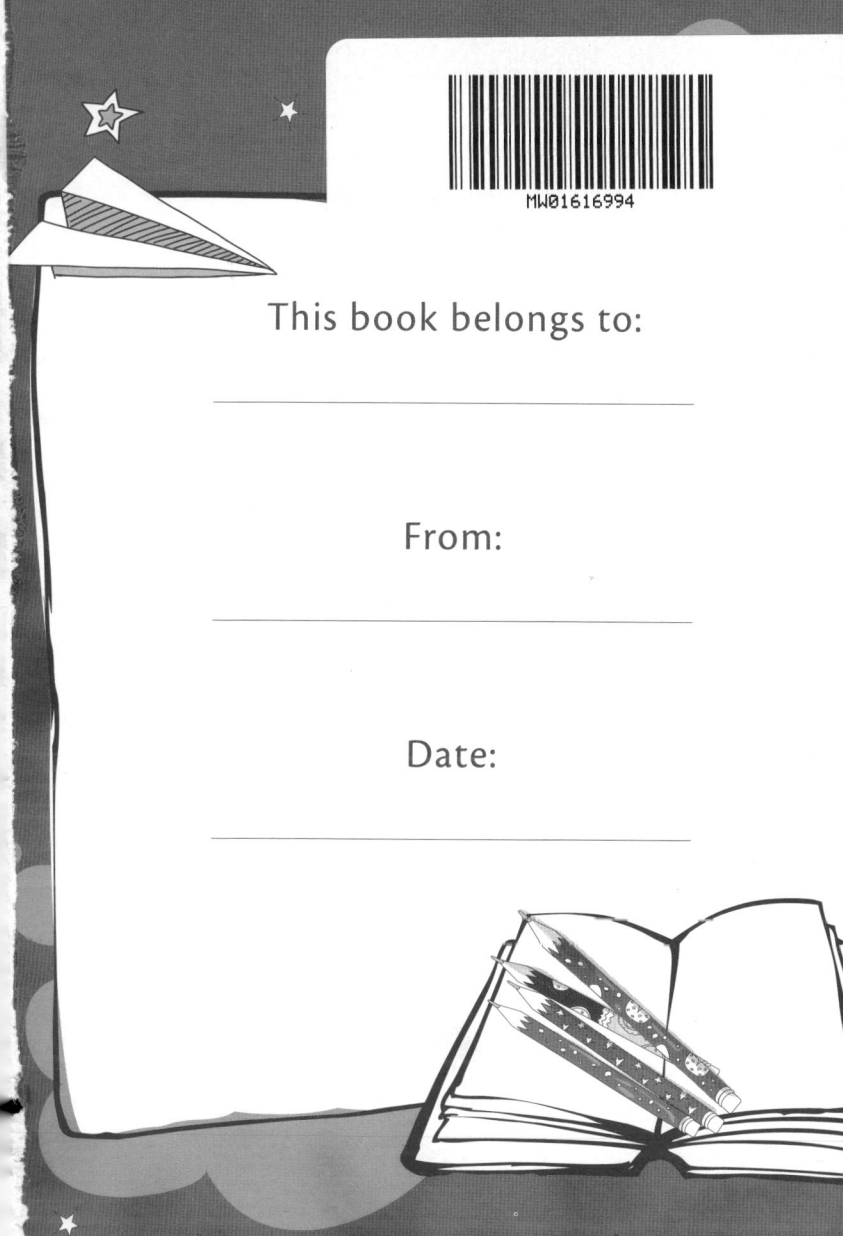

This book belongs to:

_____

From:

_____

Date:

_____

77 Wise Words from Proverbs Every Kid Should Know

Copyright © 2025 by Christian Art Publishers,
PostNet Suite # 132, Private Bag X3706, Three Rivers, 1935, South Africa

© 2025
First edition 2025

Designed by Christian Art Publishers

Images used under license from Shutterstock.com

Scripture quotations marked NIV are taken from the *Holy Bible*,
New International Version®, NIV® Copyright © 1973, 1978, 1984, 2011
by Biblica, Inc.® Used by permission of Zondervan.
All rights reserved worldwide. www.zondervan.com

Scripture quotations marked NLT are taken from the *Holy Bible*, New Living Translation,
copyright © 1996, 2004, 2015 by Tyndale House Foundation. Used by permission of
Tyndale House Publishers, Carol Stream, Illinois 60188. All rights reserved.

Scriptures quotations marked ICB are quoted from
the International Children's Bible®, copyright ©1986, 1988, 1999, 2015
by Tommy Nelson. Used by permission.

Scripture quotations marked CEV are from the Contemporary English Version.
Copyright © 1991, 1992, 1995 by American Bible Society. Used by permission.

Printed in China

ISBN 978-0-638-00425-0

25   26   27   28   29   30   31   32   33   34   –   10   9   8   7   6   5   4   3   2   1

Printed in Shenzhen, China
August 2025
Print Run: PUR405526

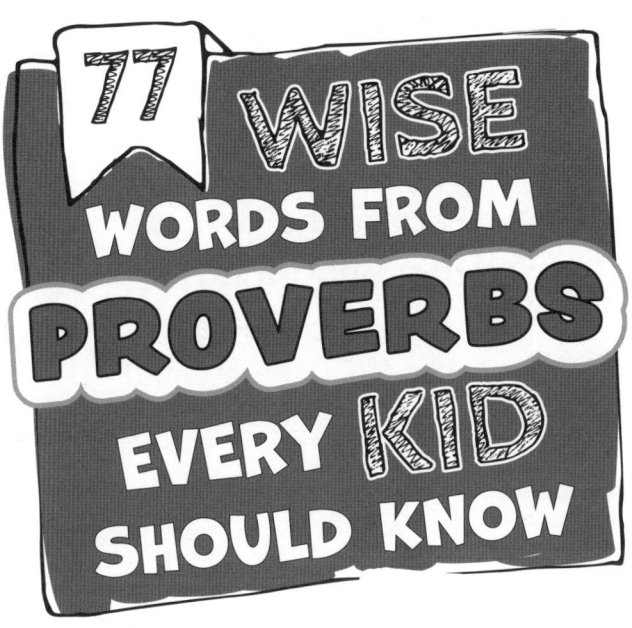

77 WISE WORDS FROM PROVERBS EVERY KID SHOULD KNOW

Christian Art
PUBLISHERS

Read it...

Fear of the LORD is
the foundation of
true knowledge.

Proverbs 1:7 NLT

Write it...

_____

_____

_____

_____

_____

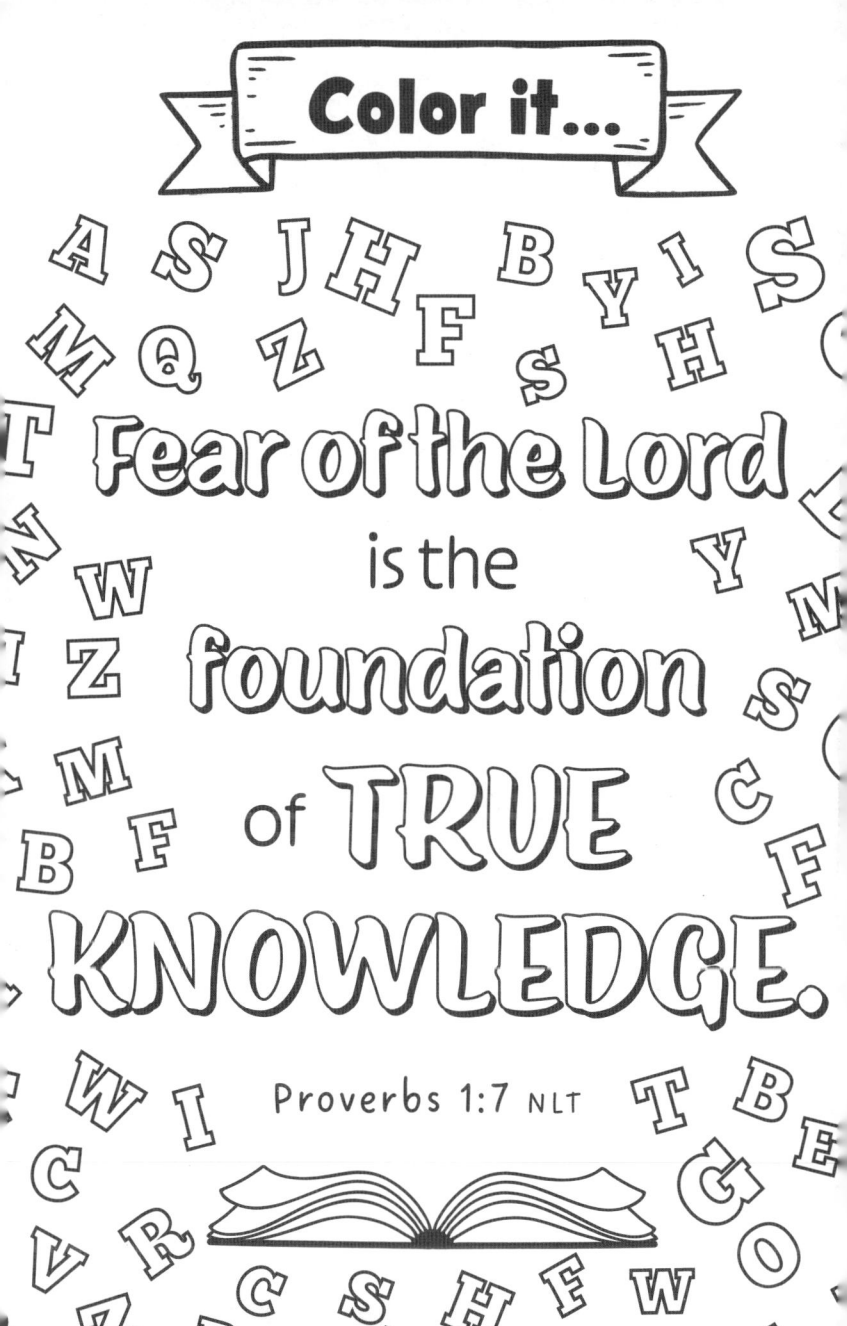

Read it...

My child, listen to
your father's teaching.
And do not forget
your mother's advice.

Proverbs 1:8 ICB

Write it...

Color it...

My child, listen to your father's teaching. And do not forget your mother's advice.

Proverbs 1:8 ICB

Read it...

Trust in the LORD with all
your heart and lean not on
your own understanding.

Proverbs 3:5 NIV

Write it...

_____

_____

_____

_____

_____

Color it...

TRUST in the LORD with all your heart

and lean not on your own understanding.

Proverbs 3:5 NIV

Read it...

As a tree makes fruit,
wisdom gives life to those
who use it. Everyone who
uses wisdom will be happy.

Proverbs 3:18 ICB

Write it...

Color it...

Do not withhold
GOOD
from those who
deserve it
when it's in your
POWER
to help them.

Proverbs 3:27 NLT

Read it...

The path of the righteous
is like the morning sun,
shining ever brighter till
the full light of day.

Proverbs 4:18 NIV

Write it...

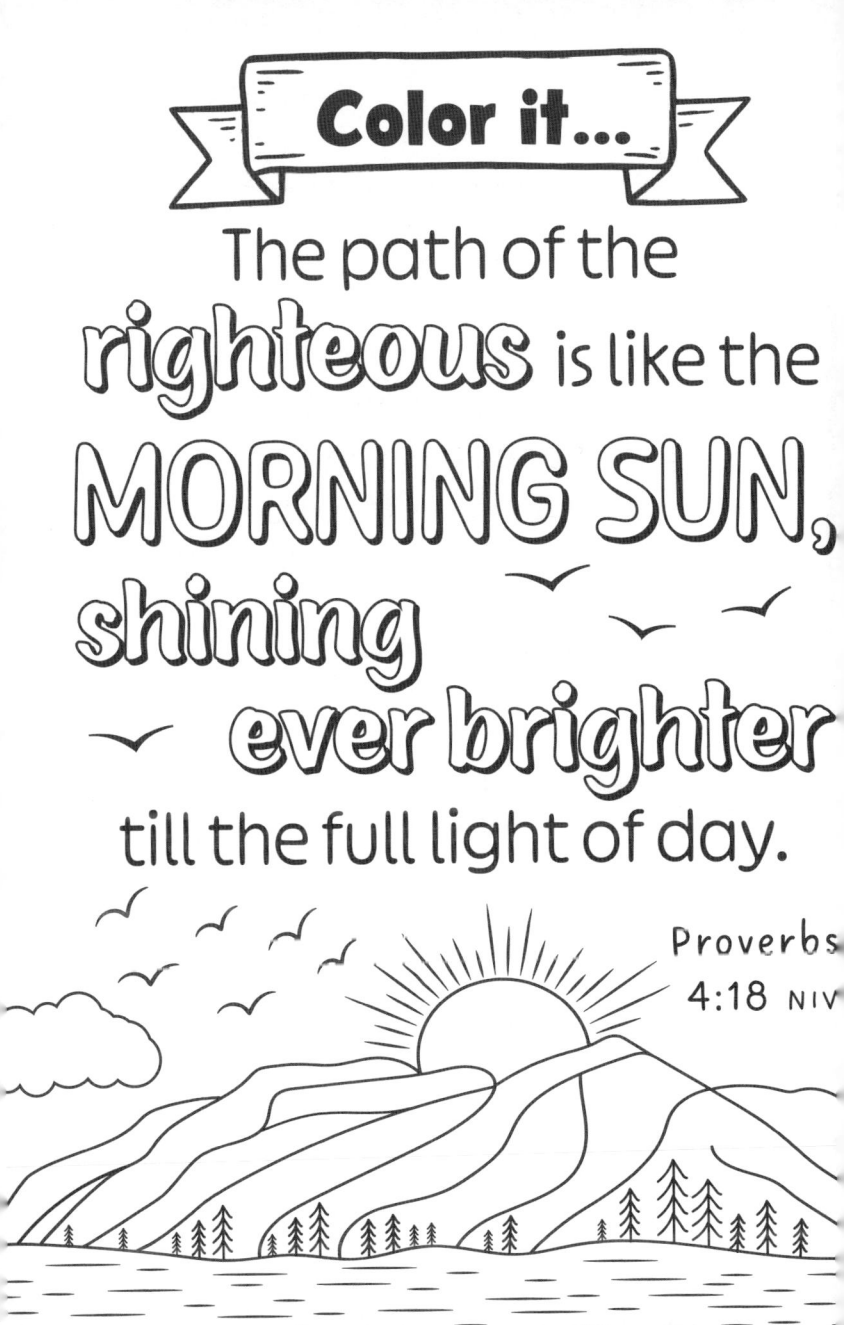

Read it...

Above all else,
guard your heart,
for everything
you do flows from it.

Proverbs 4:27 NIV

Write it...

Color it...

Above all else,

♡ GUARD ♡

your heart,

for everything

you do FLOWS

FROM IT.

Proverbs 4:27 NIV

Read it...

Keep your eyes focused
on what is right.
Keep looking straight
ahead to what is good.

Proverbs 4:25 ICB

Write it...

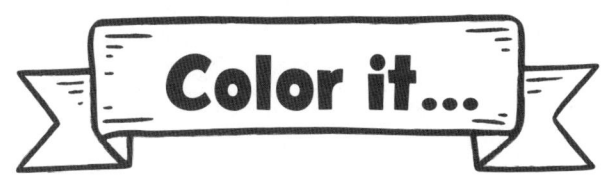

Color it...

Keep your eyes **focused** on what is **RIGHT.**

Keep looking

straight ahead to what is **GOOD.**

Proverbs 4:25 ICB

Read it...

Lazy people can learn
by watching an anthill.
Ants don't have leaders,
but they store up food
during harvest season.

Proverbs 6:6-8 CEV

Write it...

Color it...

Lazy people can learn by **watching an anthill.** Ants don't have **LEADERS,** but they **store up food** during **HARVEST SEASON.**

Proverbs 6:6-8 CEV

Read it...

Respect and obey the LORD!
This is the beginning of wisdom.

Proverbs 9:10 CEV

Write it...

Color it...

RESPECT
and
OBEY
the LORD!
This is the
beginning of
wisdom.

Proverbs 9:10 CEV

Read it...

Accept correction,
and you will find life;
reject correction,
and you will miss the road.

Proverbs 10:17 CEV

Write it...

_____

_____

_____

_____

_____

Color it...

ACCEPT
CORRECTION,
and you will find
LIFE;
reject correction,
and you will
miss the road.

Proverbs 10:17 CEV

Read it...

If you obey the Lord,
you will always know the
right thing to say. But no one
will trust you if you tell lies.

Proverbs 10:32 CEV

Write it...

_____

_____

_____

_____

_____

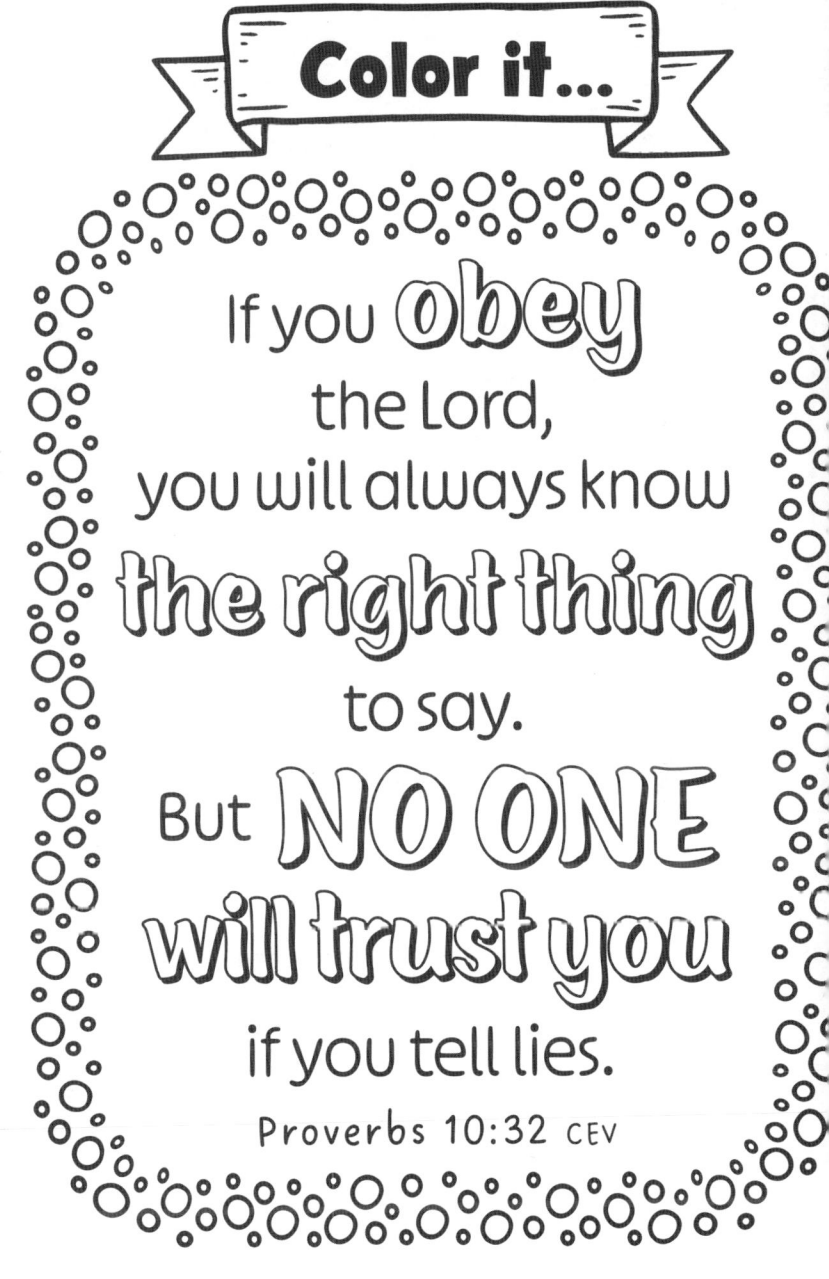

Read it...

> The generous will prosper;
> those who refresh others will
> themselves be refreshed.
>
> *Proverbs 11:25 NLT*

Write it...

_____

_____

_____

_____

_____

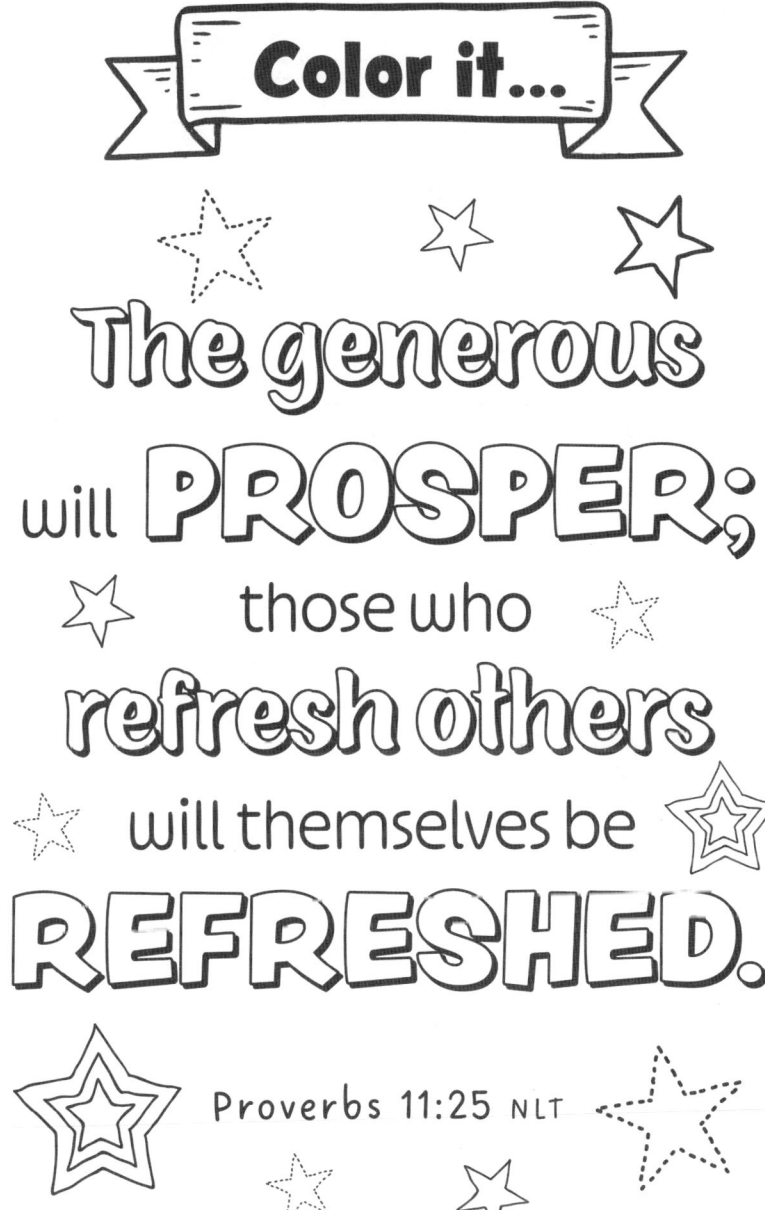

Color it...

The generous will **PROSPER;** those who refresh others will themselves be **REFRESHED.**

Proverbs 11:25 NLT

Read it...

The righteous care for
the needs of their animals.

Proverbs 12:10 NIV

Write it...

_____

_____

_____

_____

_____

Read it...

A hard worker has plenty of food,
but a person who chases
fantasies has no sense.

Proverbs 12:11 NLT

Write it...

Color it...

A hard worker
has
PLENTY OF FOOD,
but a person
who chases fantasies
has no sense.

Proverbs 12:11 NLT

Read it...

Wise words bring many benefits,
and hard work brings rewards.

Proverbs 12:14 NLT

Write it...

_____

_____

_____

_____

_____

34

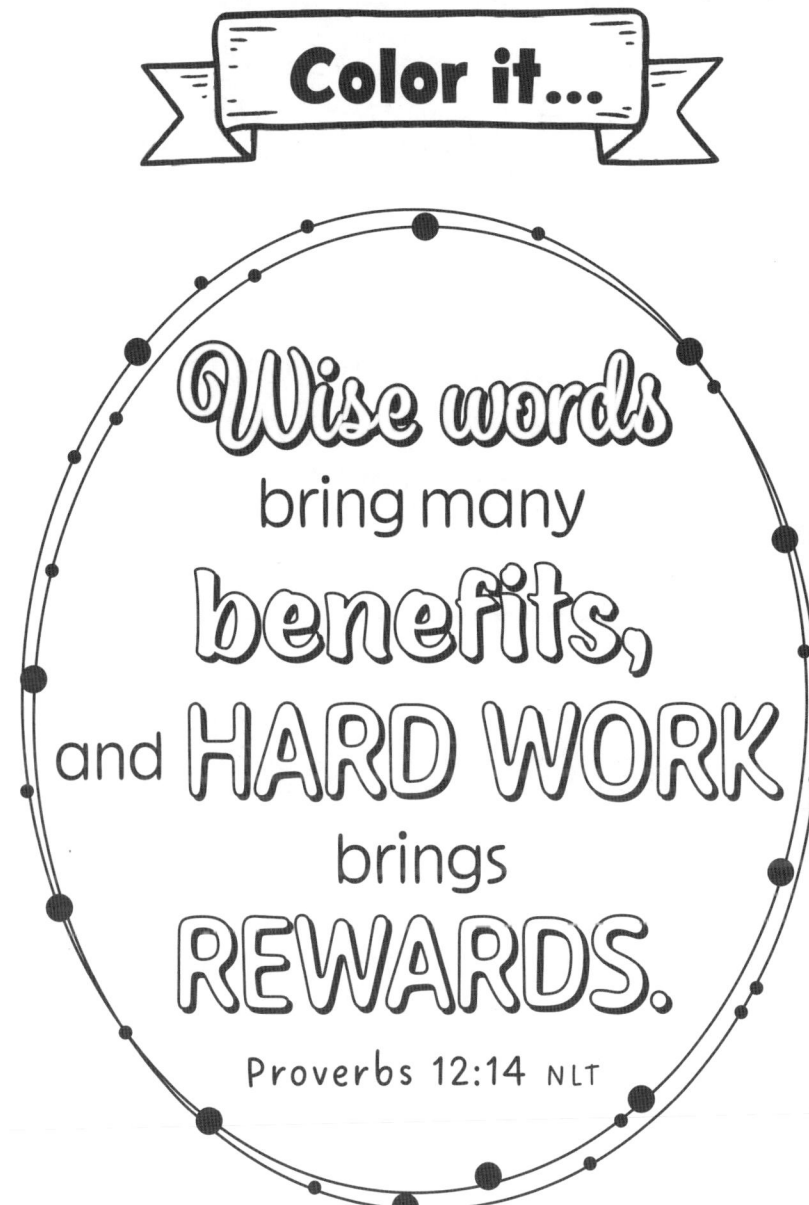

Read it...

Live right, and you are safe!
But sin will destroy you.

Proverbs 13:6 CEV

Write it...

Color it...

LIVE RIGHT,

and you are

safe!

But sin

will destroy you.

Proverbs 13:6 CEV

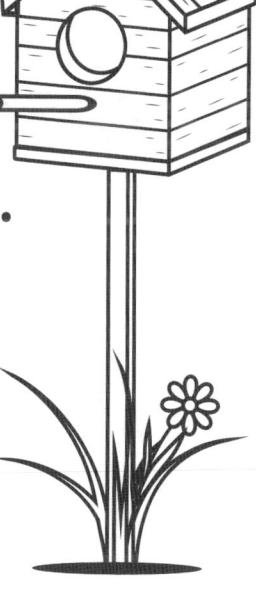

Read it...

Pride leads to arguments.
But those who
take advice are wise.

Proverbs 13:10 ICB

Write it...

Color it...

PRIDE
leads to
arguments.
But those who
take advice
are WISE.

Proverbs 13:10 ICB

Read it...

If you reject God's teaching,
you will pay the price;
if you obey His commands,
you will be rewarded.

Proverbs 13:13 CEV

Write it...

Color it...

If you reject **God's teaching,** you will pay the price; if you **OBEY** **His commands,** you will be **REWARDED.**

Proverbs 13:13 CEV

Read it...

Walk with the wise
and become wise;
associate with fools
and get in trouble.

Proverbs 13:20 NLT

Write it...

_____

_____

_____

_____

_____

Color it...

WALK
with the
wise and
become wise;
associate with fools
and get in trouble.

Proverbs 13:20 NLT

Read it...

By living right,
you show that you
respect the LORD.

Proverbs 14:2 CEV

Write it...

_____

_____

_____

_____

_____

Color it...

By

LIVING RIGHT,

you show

that you

respect

the LORD.

Proverbs 14:2 CEV

Read it...

You harvest what you plant,
whether good or bad.

Proverbs 14:14 CEV

Write it...

_____

_____

_____

_____

_____

Color it...

You
HARVEST
what you
plant,
whether
GOOD
or bad.

Proverbs 14:14 CEV

Read it...

Whoever fears the LORD
has a secure fortress,
and for their children
it will be a refuge.

Proverbs 14:26 NIV

Write it...

Color it...

Whoever **fears**
THE LORD has a
SECURE FORTRESS,
and for
their children
it will be a
refuge.

Proverbs
14:26 NIV

Read it...

Godliness makes a nation great,
but sin is a disgrace to any people.

Proverbs 14:34 NLT

Write it...

Color it...

Godliness makes A NATION great, but sin is a disgrace to ANY PEOPLE.

Proverbs 14:34 NLT

Read it...

As a tree gives us fruit,
healing words give us life.
But evil words crush the spirit.

Proverbs 15:4 ICB

Write it...

Color it...

As a **tree** gives us **fruit,** **healing words** give us **life.**

But evil words crush the spirit.

Proverbs 15:4 ICB

Read it...

A simple meal with love
is better than a feast
where there is hatred.

Proverbs 15:17 CEV

Write it...

_____

_____

_____

_____

_____

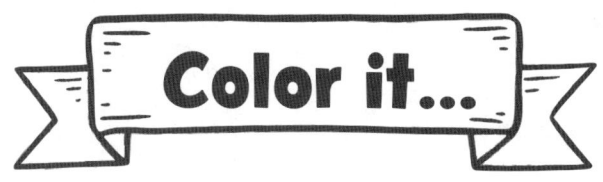

Color it...

A simple meal with *love* is **BETTER** than a feast where there is hatred.

Proverbs 15:17 CEV

Read it...

A cheerful look brings
joy to the heart;
good news makes
for good health.

Proverbs 15:30 NLT

Write it...

Color it...

A cheerful look
brings *joy* to the

♡ *heart;* ♡
good news
makes for

GOOD HEALTH.

♡ Proverbs 15:30 NLT ♡

Read it...

Showing respect to the LORD
will make you wise,
and being humble
will bring honor to you.

Proverbs 15:33 CEV

Write it...

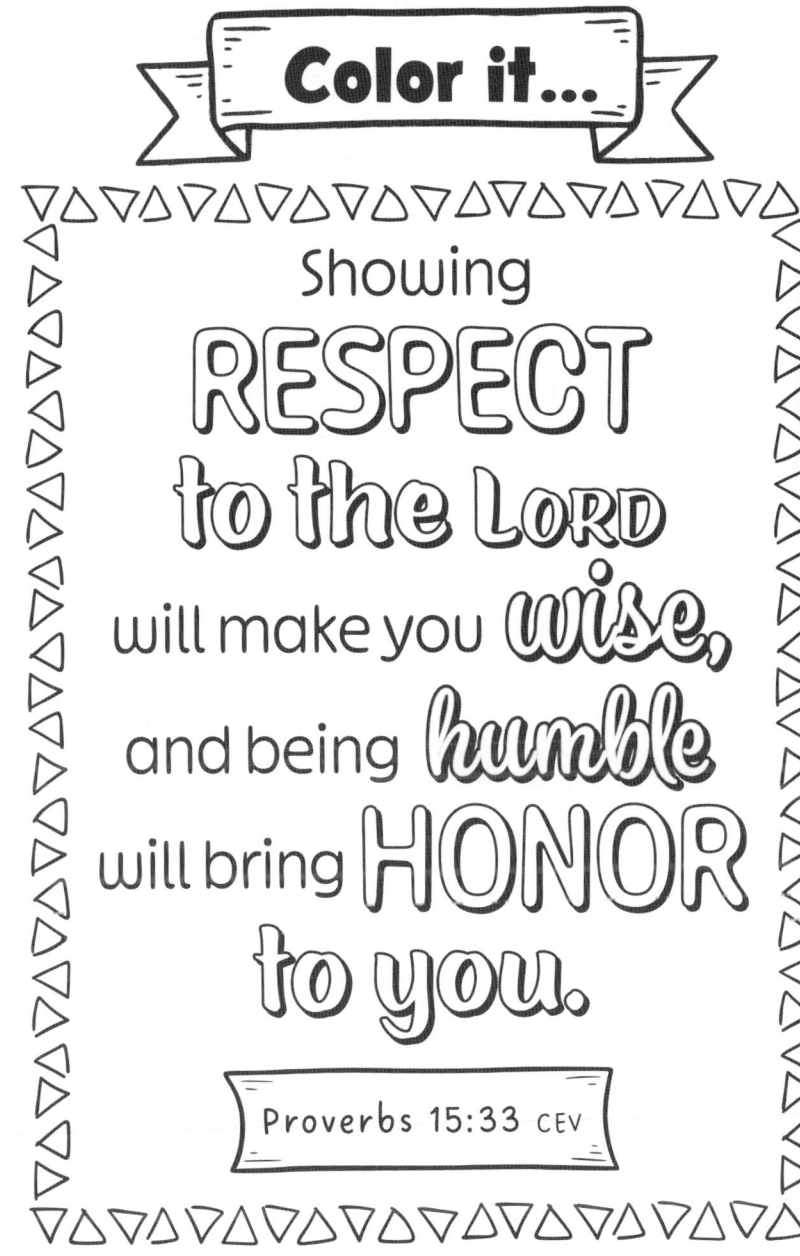

Color it...

Showing
RESPECT
to the Lord
will make you *wise,*
and being *humble*
will bring HONOR
to you.

Proverbs 15:33 CEV

Read it...

People make plans in their hearts.
But only the Lord can make
those plans come true.

Proverbs 16:1 ICB

Write it...

Color it...

People make plans in

their

hearts.

But only

the Lord

can make

THOSE PLANS

come true.

Proverbs 16:1 ICB

Read it...

Commit to the LORD
whatever you do,
and He will establish
your plans.

Proverbs 16:3 NIV

Write it...

Color it...

Commit
to the Lord
whatever you do,
and He will
ESTABLISH
YOUR PLANS.

Proverbs 16:3 NIV

Read it...

Better to have little,
with godliness,
than to be rich
and dishonest.

Proverbs 16:8 NLT

Write it...

_____

_____

_____

_____

_____

Read it...

Those who listen to
instruction will prosper;
those who trust the
LORD will be joyful.

Proverbs 16:20 NLT

Write it...

Read it...

Gracious words are a honeycomb,
sweet to the soul and
healing to the bones.

Proverbs 16:24 NIV

Write it...

Color it...

Gracious words
are a
HONEYCOMB,
sweet to the soul 
and *healing* 
to the bones.

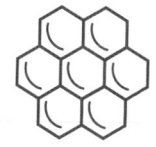

Proverbs 16:24 NIV

Read it...

Patience is better than strength.
Controlling your temper is
better than capturing a city.

Proverbs 16:32 ICB

Write it...

_____

_____

_____

_____

_____

Color it...

Patience is better than STRENGTH. Controlling your temper is better than capturing a city.

Proverbs 16:32 ICB

Read it...

It is better to eat a dry crust
of bread in peace than to have
a feast where there is quarreling.

Proverbs 17:1 ICB

Write it...

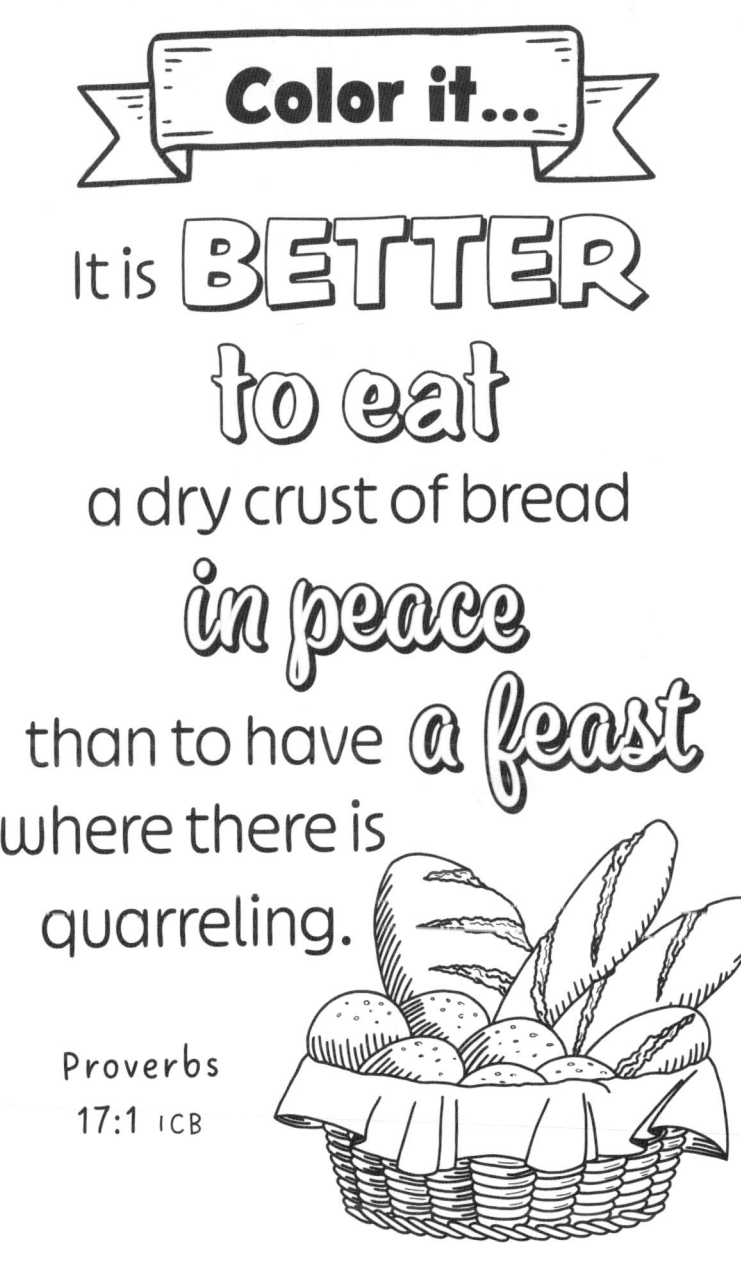

Color it...

It is **BETTER** to eat a dry crust of bread *in peace* than to have *a feast* where there is quarreling.

Proverbs 17:1 ICB

Read it...

Fire tests the purity
of silver and gold,
but the Lord tests the heart.

Proverbs 17:3 NLT

Write it...

Color it...

FIRE

tests

the purity

of silver and gold,

but **THE LORD**

tests

the heart.

Proverbs
17:3 NLT

Read it...

Grandparents are proud
of their grandchildren,
and children should be
proud of their parents.

Proverbs 17:6 CEV

Write it...

Color it...

GRANDPARENTS are *proud* of their GRANDCHILDREN, and CHILDREN should be *proud* of their PARENTS.

Proverbs 17:6 CEV

Read it...

You will always have trouble
if you are mean to those
who are good to you.

Proverbs 17:13 CEV

Write it...

Color it...

You will *always* have **trouble** if you are mean to those who are

GOOD

to you.

Proverbs 17:13 CEV

Read it...

A friend is there to help,
in any situation,
and relatives are born
to share our troubles.

Proverbs 17:17 CEV

Write it...

Color it...

A friend is there to **HELP,** in any situation, and *relatives* are born to share our troubles.

Proverbs 17:17 CEV

Read it...

A cheerful heart
is good medicine,
but a crushed spirit
dries up the bones.

Proverbs 17:22 NIV

Write it...

Color it...

A cheerful heart is good medicine, but a crushed spirit dries up the bones.

Proverbs 17:22 NIV

Read it...

A truly wise person uses few words;
a person with understanding
is even-tempered.

Proverbs 17:27 NLT

Write it...

_____

_____

_____

_____

_____

Color it...

A truly wise person uses few words; a person with understanding is even-tempered.

Proverbs 17:27 NLT

Read it...

Wise words are like deep waters;
wisdom flows from the wise
like a bubbling brook.

Proverbs 18:4 NLT

Write it...

Color it...

WISE WORDS
are like
DEEP WATERS;
wisdom
flows from the
wise
like a
bubbling
brook.

Proverbs 18:4 NLT

Read it...

It is not good to honor the wicked.
Nor is it good to be unfair
to the innocent.

Proverbs 18:5 ICB

Write it...

_____

_____

_____

_____

_____

Color it...

It is not good
TO HONOR
the wicked.
Nor is it good
to be unfair
to the
INNOCENT.

Proverbs 18:5 ICB

Read it...

The LORD is a mighty tower
where His people can run for safety.

Proverbs 18:10 CEV

Write it...

_____

_____

_____

_____

_____

THE LORD is a
MIGHTY
TOWER
where
HIS PEOPLE
can run for
SAFETY.

Proverbs 18:10 CEV

Read it...

Pride leads to destruction;
humility leads to honor.

Proverbs 18:12 CEV

Write it...

_____

_____

_____

_____

_____

Color it...

PRIDE
leads to
destruction;

humility
leads to

HONOR.

Proverbs 18:12 CEV

46

Read it...

What you say can
mean life or death.
Those who love to talk
will be rewarded for
what they say.

Proverbs 18:21 ICB

Write it...

_____

_____

_____

_____

_____

Color it...

What you say
can mean
life or death.
Those who
love to talk
will be
rewarded
for what they say.

Proverbs 18:21 ICB

Read it...

One who has unreliable friends
soon comes to ruin,
but there is a friend who
sticks closer than a brother.

Proverbs 18:24 NIV

Write it...

Color it...

One who has
unreliable friends
soon comes to ruin,
but there is

a friend
WHO STICKS
closer than
A BROTHER.

Proverbs 18:24 NIV

Read it...

Sensible people control
their temper; they earn respect
by overlooking wrongs.

Proverbs 19:11 NLT

Write it...

Color it...

SENSIBLE PEOPLE

control their temper;
they earn

RESPECT

by overlooking

wrongs.

Proverbs
19:11 NLT

Read it...

Whoever is kind to the poor
lends to the LORD,
and He will reward them
for what they have done.

Proverbs 19:17 NIV

Write it...

Color it...

Whoever is KIND
to the poor
LENDS to the LORD,
and He will reward
them for what
they
have done.

Proverbs
19:17 NIV

Read it...

Get all the advice and
instruction you can,
so you will be wise
the rest of your life.

Proverbs 19:20 NLT

Write it...

_____

_____

_____

_____

_____

Color it...

Get all the **ADVICE** and **instruction** you can, so you will be **WISE** the rest of your life.

Proverbs 19:20 NLT

Read it...

We may make a lot of plans,
but the LORD will do
what He has decided.

Proverbs 19:21 CEV

Write it...

Color it...

We may make
a lot of plans,
but the LORD will do
what He has DECIDED.

Proverbs 19:21 CEV

Read it...

Fear of the LORD leads to life,
bringing security and
protection from harm.

Proverbs 19:23 NLT

Write it...

_____

_____

_____

_____

_____

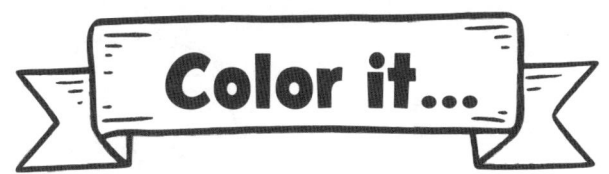

Color it...

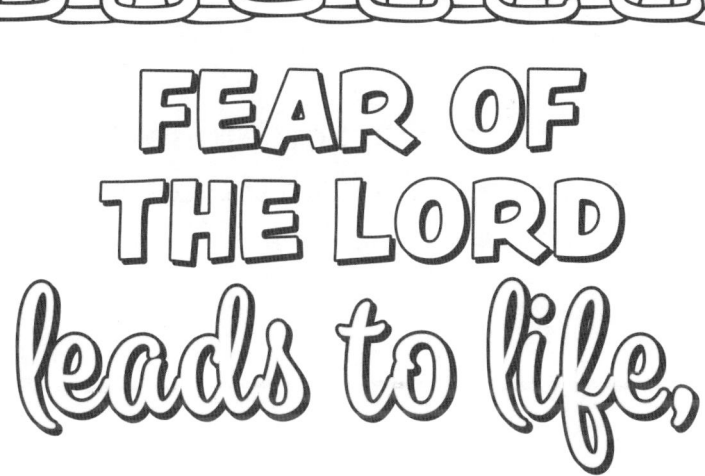

FEAR OF THE LORD leads to life, bringing SECURITY and PROTECTION from harm.

Proverbs 19:23 NLT

Read it...

Ears to hear and eyes to see—
both are gifts from the LORD.

Proverbs 20:12 NLT

Write it...

Color it...

EARS TO HEAR
and
EYES TO SEE—

both are *gifts*
from

THE LORD.

Proverbs
20:12 NLT

Read it...

Gold there is, and rubies in
abundance, but lips that speak
knowledge are a rare jewel.

Proverbs 20:15 NIV

Write it...

_____

_____

_____

_____

_____

Color it...

Gold there is,
and rubies
in abundance,
but lips that speak
KNOWLEDGE
are a
RARE
JEWEL.

Proverbs 20:15 NIV

Read it...

Don't try to get even.
Trust the LORD,
and He will help you.

Proverbs 20:22 CEV

Write it...

Read it...

Don't trap yourself by making
a rash promise to God
and only later counting the cost.

Proverbs 20:25 NLT

Write it...

_____

_____

_____

_____

_____

Color it...

Don't trap
YOURSELF
by making a rash
PROMISE TO GOD
and only later
counting
the cost.

Proverbs 20:25 NLT

Read it...

The glory of young men
is their strength,
gray hair the splendor of the old.

Proverbs 20:29 NIV

Write it...

Read it...

A person may believe
he is doing right.
But the Lord
judges his reasons.

Proverbs 21:2 ICB

Write it...

_____

_____

_____

_____

_____

Color it...

A person may
believe
he is
DOING RIGHT.
But the Lord
judges
his reasons.

Proverbs 21:2 ICB

Read it...

Wealth that comes
from telling lies
vanishes like a mist
and leads to death.

Proverbs 21:6 ICB

Write it...

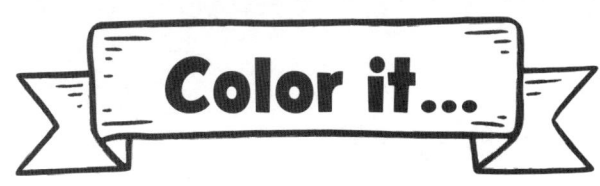
Color it...

WEALTH

that comes from
telling lies
vanishes like

a mist

and leads
to death.

Proverbs 21:6 ICB

60

Read it...

A person who tries to live right
and be loyal finds life,
success and honor.

Proverbs 21:21 ICB

Write it...

_____

_____

_____

_____

_____

Color it...

A person
who tries to **live right**
and **be loyal**
FINDS LIFE,
SUCCESS
and HONOR.

Proverbs 21:21 ICB

61

Read it...

Being respected is more important
than having great riches.
To be well thought of is better
than owning silver or gold.

Proverbs 22:1 ICB

Write it...

_____

_____

_____

_____

_____

Color it...

Being respected
is more important than
having
GREAT RICHES.
To be **well thought of**

is
BETTER

than owning
silver or gold.

Proverbs 22:1 ICB

Read it...

Respecting the Lord and
not being proud will bring
you wealth, honor and life.

Proverbs 22:4 ICB

Write it...

Color it...

RESPECTING
THE LORD
and not being proud
will bring you
WEALTH,
HONOR
AND LIFE.

Proverbs 22:4 ICB

Read it...

The generous will
themselves be blessed,
for they share their food
with the poor.

Proverbs 22:9 NIV

Write it...

Color it...

THE GENEROUS

will themselves

be blessed,

for they SHARE

their

food

with the poor.

Proverbs 22:9 NIV

Read it...

Whoever loves a pure heart
and gracious speech
will have the king as a friend.

Proverbs 22:11 NLT

Write it...

_____

_____

_____

_____

_____

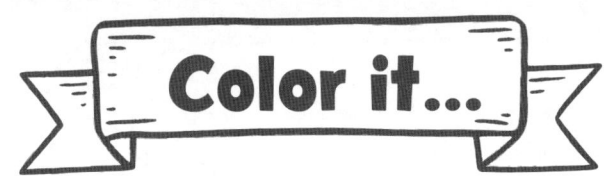
Color it...

Whoever *loves*
A PURE HEART and
GRACIOUS SPEECH
will have the
king 👑
as a *friend.*

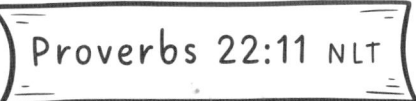
Proverbs 22:11 NLT

Read it...

Remember what you are taught.
And listen carefully to
words of knowledge.

Proverbs 23:12 ICB

Write it...

Color it...

REMEMBER
what you are
TAUGHT.
And
listen carefully
to WORDS
OF KNOWLEDGE.

Proverbs 23:12 ICB

Read it...

Don't envy sinners, but always
continue to fear the LORD.
You will be rewarded for this;
your hope will not be disappointed.

Proverbs 23:17-18 NLT

Write it...

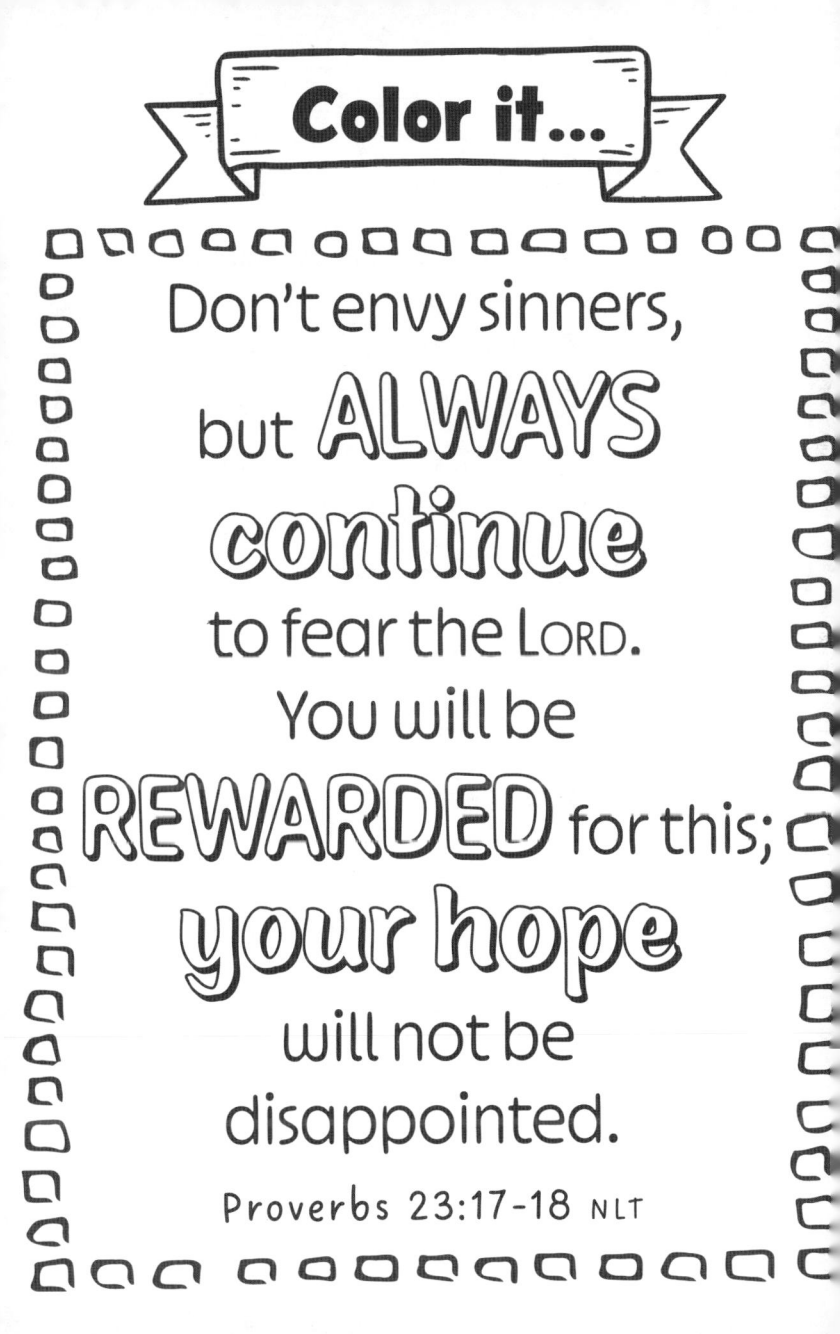

Color it...

Don't envy sinners, but ALWAYS continue to fear the LORD. You will be REWARDED for this; your hope will not be disappointed.

Proverbs 23:17-18 NLT

67

Read it...

Use wisdom and understanding
to establish your home;
let good sense fill the rooms
with priceless treasures.

Proverbs 24:3-4 CEV

Write it...

_____

_____

_____

_____

_____

Color it...

Use WISDOM and UNDERSTANDING to establish your home; let GOOD SENSE fill the rooms with priceless treasures.

Proverbs 24:3-4 CEV

68

Read it...

Honey is good for you, my children,
and it tastes sweet. Wisdom is
like honey for your life—if you
find it, your future is bright.

Proverbs 24:13-14 CEV

Write it...

Color it...

Honey is good for you, my children, and it tastes SWEET. WISDOM is like *honey* for your life— if you find it, your future is BRIGHT.

HONEY

Proverbs 24:13-14 CEV

Read it...

Do your planning and
prepare your fields
before building your house.

Proverbs 24:27 NLT

Write it...

_____

_____

_____

_____

_____

Color it...

Do your **planning** and **prepare** **your fields** before **building** **your house.**

Proverbs
24:27 NLT

Read it...

The right word spoken at the right time is as beautiful as gold apples in a silver bowl.

Proverbs 25:11 ICB

Write it...

Color it...

THE RIGHT WORD
spoken at
THE RIGHT TIME
is as *beautiful*
as GOLD APPLES
in a SILVER BOWL.

Proverbs 25:11 ICB

Read it...

Like a city whose walls are broken through is a person who lacks self-control.

Proverbs 25:28 NIV

Write it...

_____

_____

_____

_____

_____

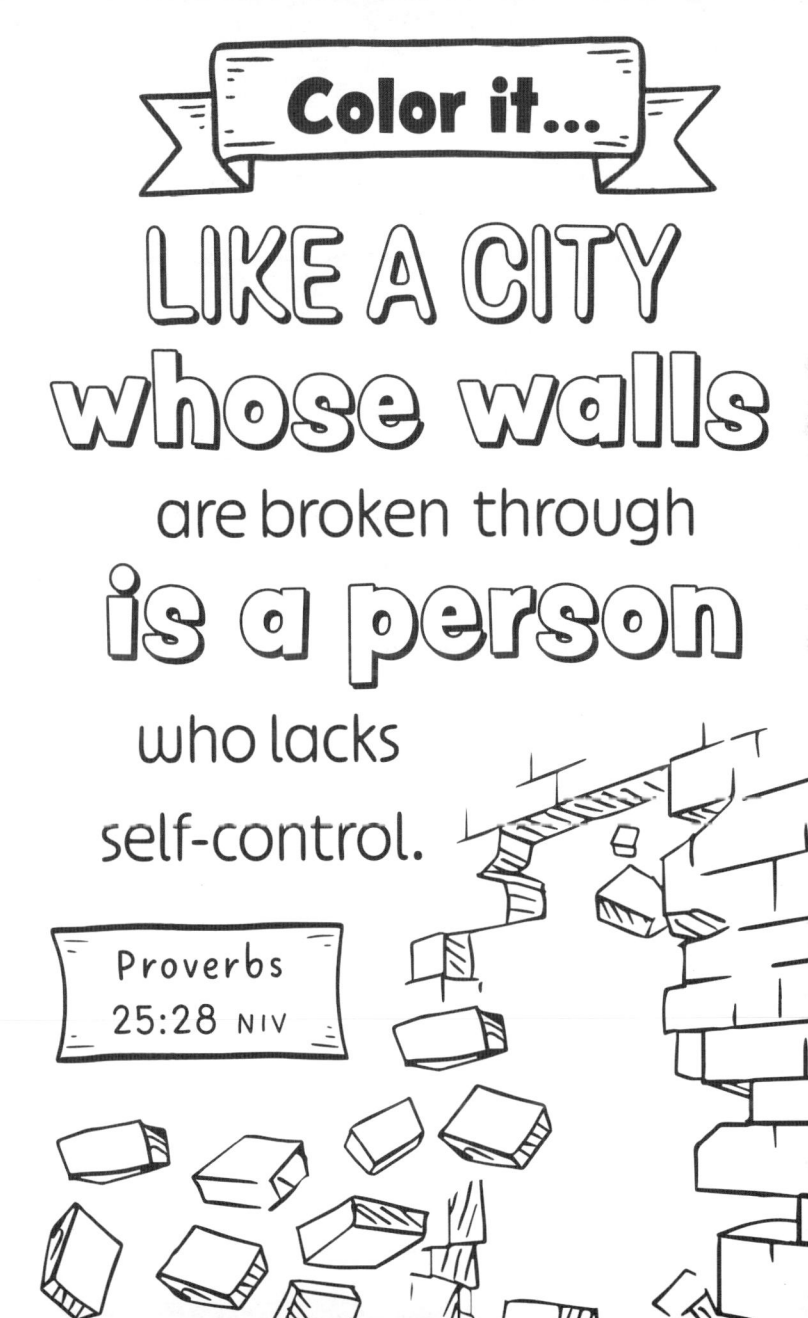

Read it...

Without wood,
a fire will go out.
And without gossip,
quarreling will stop.

Proverbs 26:20 ICB

Write it...

Color it...

Without wood, A FIRE will go out.

And without gossip, quarreling

WILL STOP.

Proverbs
26:20 ICB

Read it...

Don't brag about yourself—
let others praise you.

Proverbs 27:2 CEV

Write it...

Color it...

Don't brag
about yourself—
let others
praise you.

Proverbs 27:2 CEV

Read it...

"Every word of God is flawless;
He is a shield to those who
take refuge in Him."

Proverbs 30:5 NIV

Write it...

_____

_____

_____

_____

_____

Color it...

"EVERY WORD OF GOD is flawless; He is a SHIELD to those who take REFUGE in Him."

Proverbs 30:5 NIV

Read it...

If you hide your sins,
you will not succeed.
If you confess and reject them,
you will receive mercy.

Proverbs 28:13 ICB

Write it...

Color it...

If you hide your sins,
you will not succeed.
If you **confess**
and reject them,
you will **receive**
MERCY.

Proverbs 28:13 ICB

Read it...

A greedy person causes trouble.
But the one who trusts
the Lord will succeed.

Proverbs 28:25 ICB

Write it...

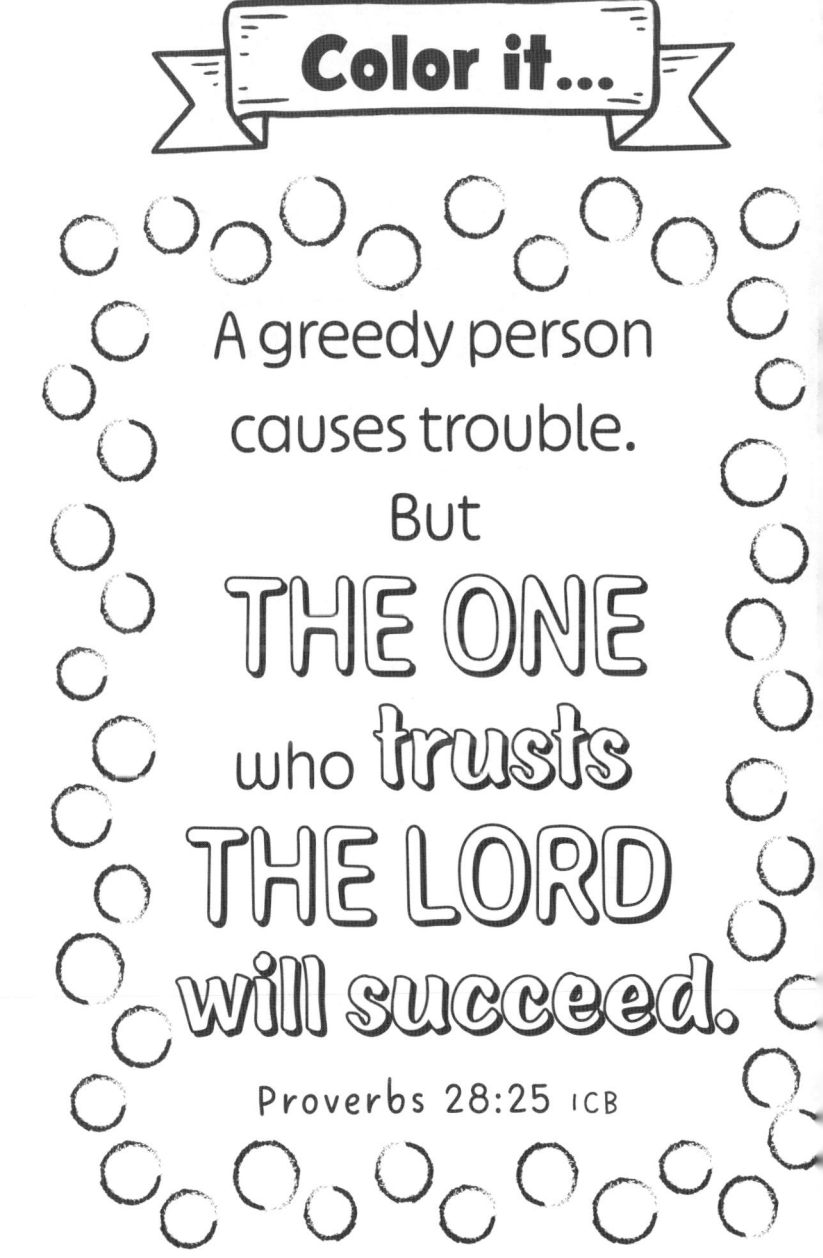

Color it...

A greedy person
causes trouble.
But
THE ONE
who **trusts**
THE LORD
will succeed.

Proverbs 28:25 ICB

77

Read it...

Speak up for those who cannot speak for themselves; ensure justice for those being crushed.

Proverbs 31:8 NLT

Write it...

Color it...

SPEAK UP

for those who cannot
speak for themselves;

ensure justice

for those
being crushed.

Proverbs
31:8 NLT

Tick the Scripture verses you've memorized

1. Fear of the LORD is the foundation of true knowledge. (Prov. 1:7 NLT) ☐
2. My child, listen to your father's teaching. And do not forget your mother's advice. (Prov. 1:8 ICB) ☐
3. Trust in the LORD with all your heart and lean not on your own understanding. (Prov. 3:5 NIV) ☐
4. As a tree makes fruit, wisdom gives life to those who use it. Everyone who uses wisdom will be happy. (Prov. 3:18 ICB) ☐
5. Do not withhold good from those who deserve it when it's in your power to help them. (Prov. 3:27 NLT) ☐
6. The path of the righteous is like the morning sun, shining ever brighter till the full light of day. (Prov. 4:18 NIV) ☐
7. Above all else, guard your heart, for everything you do flows from it. (Prov. 4:27 NIV) ☐
8. Keep your eyes focused on what is right. Keep looking straight ahead to what is good. (Prov. 4:25 ICB) ☐
9. Lazy people can learn by watching an anthill. Ants don't have leaders, but they store up food during harvest season. (Prov. 6:6-8 CEV) ☐
10. Respect and obey the LORD! This is the beginning of wisdom. (Prov. 9:10 CEV) ☐
11. Accept correction, and you will find life; reject correction, and you will miss the road. (Prov. 10:17 CEV) ☐
12. If you obey the Lord, you will always know the right thing to say. But no one will trust you if you tell lies. (Prov. 10:32 CEV) ☐
13. The generous will prosper; those who refresh others will themselves be refreshed. (Prov. 11:25 NLT) ☐
14. The righteous care for the needs of their animals. (Prov. 12:10 NIV) ☐
15. A hard worker has plenty of food, but a person who chases fantasies has no sense. (Prov. 12:11 NLT) ☐
16. Wise words bring many benefits, and hard work brings rewards. (Prov. 12:14 NLT) ☐
17. Live right, and you are safe! But sin will destroy you. (Prov. 13:6 CEV) ☐
18. Pride leads to arguments. But those who take advice are wise. (Prov. 13:10 ICB) ☐
19. If you reject God's teaching, you will pay the price; if you obey His commands, you will be rewarded. (Prov. 13:13 CEV) ☐
20. Walk with the wise and become wise; associate with fools and get in trouble. (Prov. 13:20 NLT) ☐
21. By living right, you show that you respect the LORD. (Prov. 14:2 CEV) ☐
22. You harvest what you plant, whether good or bad. (Prov. 14:14 CEV) ☐
23. Whoever fears the LORD has a secure fortress, and for their children it will be a refuge. (Prov. 14:26 NIV) ☐
24. Godliness makes a nation great, but sin is a disgrace to any people. (Prov. 14:34 NLT) ☐
25. As a tree gives us fruit, healing words give us life. But evil words crush the spirit. (Prov. 15:4 ICB) ☐
26. A simple meal with love is better than a feast where there is hatred. (Prov. 15:17 CEV) ☐

27. A cheerful look brings joy to the heart; good news makes for good health. (Prov. 15:30 NLT)
28. Showing respect to the LORD will make you wise, and being humble will bring honor to you. (Prov. 15:33 CEV)
29. People make plans in their hearts. But only the Lord can make those plans come true. (Prov. 16:1 ICB)
30. Commit to the LORD whatever you do, and He will establish your plans. (Prov. 16:3 NIV)
31. Better to have little, with godliness, than to be rich and dishonest. (Prov. 16:8 NLT)
32. Those who listen to instruction will prosper; those who trust the LORD will be joyful. (Prov. 16:20 NLT)
33. Gracious words are a honeycomb, sweet to the soul and healing to the bones. (Prov. 16:24 NIV)
34. Patience is better than strength. Controlling your temper is better than capturing a city. (Prov. 16:32 ICB)
35. It is better to eat a dry crust of bread in peace than to have a feast where there is quarreling. (Prov. 17:1 ICB)
36. Fire tests the purity of silver and gold, but the LORD tests the heart. (Prov. 17:3 NLT)
37. Grandparents are proud of their grandchildren, and children should be proud of their parents. (Prov. 17:6 CEV)
38. You will always have trouble if you are mean to those who are good to you. (Prov. 17:13 CEV)
39. A friend is there to help, in any situation, and relatives are born to share our troubles. (Prov. 17:17 CEV)
40. A cheerful heart is good medicine, but a crushed spirit dries up the bones. (Prov. 17:22 NIV)
41. A truly wise person uses few words; a person with understanding is even-tempered. (Prov. 17:27 NLT)
42. Wise words are like deep waters; wisdom flows from the wise like a bubbling brook. (Prov. 18:4 NLT)
43. It is not good to honor the wicked. Nor is it good to be unfair to the innocent. (Prov. 18:5 ICB)
44. The LORD is a mighty tower where His people can run for safety. (Prov. 18:10 CEV)
45. Pride leads to destruction; humility leads to honor. (Prov. 18:12 CEV)
46. What you say can mean life or death. Those who love to talk will be rewarded for what they say. (Prov. 18:21 ICB)
47. One who has unreliable friends soon comes to ruin, but there is a friend who sticks closer than a brother. (Prov. 18:24 NIV)
48. Sensible people control their temper; they earn respect by overlooking wrongs. (Prov. 19:11 NLT)
49. Whoever is kind to the poor lends to the LORD, and He will reward them for what they have done. (Prov. 19:17 NIV)
50. Get all the advice and instruction you can, so you will be wise the rest of your life. (Prov. 19:20 NLT)
51. We may make a lot of plans, but the LORD will do what He has decided. (Prov. 19:21 CEV)
52. Fear of the LORD leads to life, bringing security and protection from harm. (Prov. 19:23 NLT)

Ears to hear and eyes to see—both are gifts from the Lord. (Prov. 20:12 NLT) ☐

Gold there is, and rubies in abundance, but lips that speak knowledge are a rare jewel. (Prov. 20:15 NIV) ☐

Don't try to get even. Trust the Lord, and He will help you. (Prov. 20:22 CEV) ☐

Don't trap yourself by making a rash promise to God and only later counting the cost. (Prov. 20:25 NLT) ☐

The glory of young men is their strength, gray hair the splendor of the old. (Prov. 20:29 NIV) ☐

A person may believe he is doing right. But the Lord judges his reasons. (Prov. 21:2 ICB) ☐

Wealth that comes from telling lies vanishes like a mist and leads to death. (Prov. 21:6 ICB) ☐

A person who tries to live right and be loyal finds life, success and honor. (Prov. 21:21 ICB) ☐

Being respected is more important than having great riches. To be well thought of is better than owning silver or gold. (Prov. 22:1 ICB) ☐

Respecting the Lord and not being proud will bring you wealth, honor and life. (Prov. 22:4 ICB) ☐

The generous will themselves be blessed, for they share their food with the poor. (Prov. 22:9 NIV) ☐

Whoever loves a pure heart and gracious speech will have the king as a friend. (Prov. 22:11 NLT) ☐

Remember what you are taught. And listen carefully to words of knowledge. (Prov. 23:12 ICB) ☐

Don't envy sinners, but always continue to fear the Lord. You will be rewarded for this; your hope will not be disappointed. (Prov. 23:17-18 NLT) ☐

Use wisdom and understanding to establish your home; let good sense fill the rooms with priceless treasures. (Prov. 24:3-4 CEV) ☐

Honey is good for you, my children, and it tastes sweet. Wisdom is like honey for your life— if you find it, your future is bright. (Prov. 24:13-14 CEV) ☐

Do your planning and prepare your fields before building your house. (Prov. 24:27 NLT) ☐

The right word spoken at the right time is as beautiful as gold apples in a silver bowl. (Prov. 25:11 ICB) ☐

Like a city whose walls are broken through is a person who lacks self-control. (Prov. 25:28 NIV) ☐

Without wood, a fire will go out. And without gossip, quarreling will stop. (Prov. 26:20 ICB) ☐

Don't brag about yourself—let others praise you. (Prov. 27:2 CEV) ☐

"Every word of God is flawless; He is a shield to those who take refuge in Him." (Prov. 30:5 NIV) ☐

If you hide your sins, you will not succeed. If you confess and reject them, you will receive mercy. (Prov. 28:13 ICB) ☐

A greedy person causes trouble. But the one who trusts the Lord will succeed. (Prov. 28:25 ICB) ☐

Speak up for those who cannot speak for themselves; ensure justice for those being crushed. (Prov. 31:8 NLT) ☐